Title

Teenage Cooking Recipe

By

Janty Jonah

Fried Bologna Sandwiches

1) Bologna (3 slices)
2) Bread (2 slices)
3) Butter (1 spoon)
4) Lettice (2 slices)
5) Tomatoes (2 slices)
6) Frying Pan

Toppings are your preferences

Put the frying pan on the stove, turn on the stove medium temperature. Add the butter in the frying pan, wait 10 seconds then add the Bologna. Stir the Bologna for 2 minutes then turn off the stove. Toast the slice bread in the toaster gently light. Add the Bologna on the bread, add slice Lettice then add the sliced tomatoes.

Dressing is optional

Noodles with Hotdog Chunks

1) Ramen Noodles
2) Hotdog (chopped)
3) Oil (2 spoon)
4) Ramen Noodle Seasoning (1/2)
5) Water (4 cups)
6) Pot
7) Frying Pan

Turn on the stove on medium temperature, add water in the pot, add the Ramen noodles then add the seasoning that came inside the package. Let it boil for 10 minutes then turn off the stove. Use a frying pan to fry the chopped hotdogs, turn on the stove on low temperature then add the oil in the frying pan. Add the hotdog chunks then stir for about 3 minutes. Add the Ramen noodles into the frying pan. Stir for 5 minutes then turn off the stove.

Chicken Noodle Soup

1) Boneless Chicken 4 Strips (cut into cubes)
2) Ramen Noodles (1 bag)
3) Water (10 cups)
4) Chicken Broth (1 cup)
5) Oil (1 spoon)
6) Carrots (1 cup peeled & chopped)
7) Fresh Parsley (1 cup chopped)
8) Salt (1/3 spoon)
9) Large Pot

Simple instructions

Add all the ingredients into a large pot, place the pot on the stove then turn on the stove on low temperature. Let it cook for 45 minutes then turn off the stove.

Let it cool for 20 minutes before serving

(Substitute for noodles is 1 cup of rice)

Bagel Pizza

1) Bagel (4 slices)
2) Cheese (1/2 cup)
3) Pepperoni (1 cup)
4) Butter (1 spoon)
5) Tomato Sauce (1/2 cup)
6) Baking Pan

Spread the butter on the bagels, add the sauce on top, add the pepperoni on top then add the cheese on top. Place them on the baking pan then put them into the oven. Turn on the oven on 375 degrees and allow it to bake for 15 minutes then turn off the oven.

Hotdog Sandwiches

1) 2 Hotdogs
2) ½ Onions (chopped)
3) A Pinch of Salt
4) 2 Hotdog Buns
5) Oil (1/2 cup)
6) Ketchup (2 spoon)
7) Frying Pan

Turn on the stove on medium temperature then place the frying pan on the stove. Add the oil, wait 5 seconds then add the 2 hotdogs. Stir for 5 seconds then add the onions and the salt. Stir for 5 minutes then turn off the stove.

Put each hotdog inside each bun, add onions on top then add ketchup.

Scrambled Basil Eggs

1) 3 Eggs
2) 2 strings of Basil (chopped)
3) A Pinch of Salt
4) Bowl
5) Frying Pan

Crack the eggs in a bowl then add salt. Batter the eggs for 2 minutes. Use a frying pan, turn on the stove on medium temperature. Add the oil in the pan then wait 5 seconds. Add the battered eggs then add the chopped basil. Stir for 2 minutes then turn off the stove.

Salad

1) Lettice (sliced)
2) 3 Tomatoes (sliced)
3) 1 Cucumber (chopped)
4) 2 Carrots (peeled/chopped)
5) 3 Eggs (sliced)
6) Water (4 cup)
7) Pot
8) Large Salad Bowl

Turn on the stove on high temperature, add the water in to the pot then add the eggs. Let it boil for 10 minutes then turn off the stove. Add all the vegetables inside the salad bowl. Crack and peel the eggs once they're cool then slice them. Put them on top of the salad and serve with the dressing of your choice.

Baked Potatoes

1) 2 Potatoes
2) Sour Cream (2 spoon)
3) Butter (1 spoon)
4) Cheese (1/2 cup)
5) Foil Paper
6) Baking Pan

Rinse out 2 potatoes then cover them with foil papers and place them in a baking pan. Turn on the oven on 375 degrees and put the baking pan inside the oven for 45 minutes then turn off the oven. Let the potatoes cool then cut them in the middle to put the butter, the sour cream and the cheese on top.

The skin of the potato is eatable

Oatmeal Breakfast

1) 1 cup of Oatmeal
2) 4 cups of Water
3) ½ of Milk
4) ½ spoon of Butter
5) 2 spoons of Brown Sugar

Turn on the stove on medium temperature then place the pot on the stove. Add the water, add the oatmeal, add the milk, add the butter then add the brown sugar. Cook for 10 minutes the let it cool.

Rice and Pork Beans

1) 2 bags of Instant Rice
2) 1 Can of precooked Pork Bean
3) 4 cups of Water
4) A pinch of Salt
5) 2 Pots

Place 2 pots on each stove then turn them on medium temperature. Add water in one pot and add the pork beans into the other. Boil the water for 10 minutes then turn off the stove. Add the rice bags into the hot water. Do not rip the bags. Leave them in the pot for 5 minutes then remove them out of the pot. Let the rice cool for 5 minutes then ripped the bags and pour the rice on a plate. Heat the pork beans for 5 minutes then pour them on top of the rice. Turn off the stove!

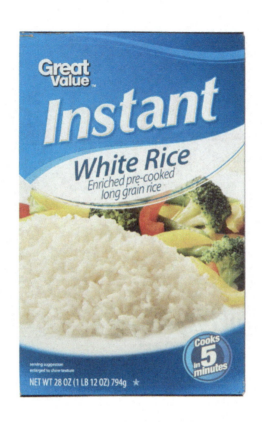

Bacon Dog

1) 3 Hotdogs
2) 3 sliced Bacon
3) Baking Pan

Turn on the oven to 375 degrees. Wrap each hotdog with the sliced bacon then place them on the baking pan. Put the baking pan into the oven and allow them to bake for 30 minutes. Check on them every 15 minutes to turn them over. Turn off the oven when they're finish and let them cool.

Thank You

*

*

*

*

*

*

*

*

*

*

*

*

*

*

*

The End

*

*

Made in the USA
Columbia, SC
26 November 2022